# Escape Fire

LESSONS FOR THE FUTURE OF HEALTH CARE

Donald M. Berwick, MD, MPP

PRESIDENT AND CEO

INSTITUTE FOR HEALTHCARE IMPROVEMENT

THE COMMONWEALTH FUND

NEW YORK, NEW YORK

The site of the Mann Gulch fire, which is described in this book, is listed
in the National Register of Historic Places. Because many regard it as sacred ground,
it is actively protected and managed by the Forest Service as a cultural landscape.

*Escape Fire* is an edited version of the Plenary Address delivered
at the Institute for Healthcare Improvement's 11th Annual National Forum
on Quality Improvement in Health Care,
in New Orleans, Louisiana, on December 9, 1999.

Published in 2002 by The Commonwealth Fund,
One East 75th Street, New York, New York 10021-2692.

*Book Design*: Landesberg Design Associates, Pittsburgh

*Photography*: Imagebank/Photodisk (cover), Paul B. Batalden (page 7),
USDA Forest Service (page 8), Eric Carlson (pages 14–15),
Donald M. Berwick (page 36), Steve Starr for Corbis/SABA (pages 48–49)

*Printing*: Broudy Printing Inc., Pittsburgh

ISBN 1-884533-00-0

On December 9, 1999, the nearly 3,000 individuals who attended the 11th Annual National Forum on Quality Improvement in Health Care heard an extraordinary address by Dr. Donald M. Berwick, the founder, president, and CEO of the Institute for Healthcare Improvement, the forum's sponsor. Entitled *Escape Fire*, Dr. Berwick's speech took its audience back to the year 1949, when a wildfire broke out on a Montana hillside, taking the lives of 13 young men and changing the way firefighting was managed in the United States. After retelling this harrowing tale, Dr. Berwick applied the lessons learned from this catastrophe to the health care system—a system that, he believes, is on the verge of its own conflagration.

One of the three men who survived the Montana fire did so through an ingenious solution and a leap of faith —by making an escape fire. Dr. Berwick suggests that the current state of health care demands as extreme and dramatic an approach. To make his case, he describes the failings of the health care delivery system as they were revealed in his wife's treatment for a serious illness. Only by abandoning many of the traditional tools of health care delivery, only by opening up the system to the patients it serves and instituting a standard of excellence, he says, will the health care system be transformed.

The Commonwealth Fund is pleased to publish *Escape Fire* in its entirety. We share its vision of a health care system that is accessible to all at all times, designed from the patient's perspective, and grounded in science. This vision is consonant with the aims of The Commonwealth Fund, as set forth in "A 2020 Vision for American Health Care," and it illuminates the path for our Program on Health Care Quality Improvement.[1]

Despite enormous expenditures and sophisticated technologies, America's health care system has been rated 37th in the world.[2] We hope that *Escape Fire* will stimulate all who read it to work to change this. For the general public, this means addressing the need to provide access to care for everyone at all times, demanding safer and better care, and being willing to support the process of improvement. For those in health care delivery, it means abandoning the rhetoric that we provide the best care in the world and using our vast power and resources to redesign the system. For those who license or accredit or regulate the system, it means informing the public about health care standards and raising the bar on performance.

Ultimately, Dr. Berwick's brighter future for health care requires the courage to acknowledge the shortcomings of our current system and the will to transform it. We hope that his speech will serve as a beacon, guiding the health care system toward a brighter future.

Stephen C. Schoenbaum, MD
*Senior Vice President, The Commonwealth Fund*

[1] Davis K., Schoen C., and Schoenbaum S. "A 2020 Vision for American Health Care," *Archives of Internal Medicine*, (160)22: 3357–62, 2000.

[2] *The World Health Report 2000—Health Systems: Improving Performance*, World Health Organization, 2000.

These are the flowers of Mann Gulch. And these are the markers of death.

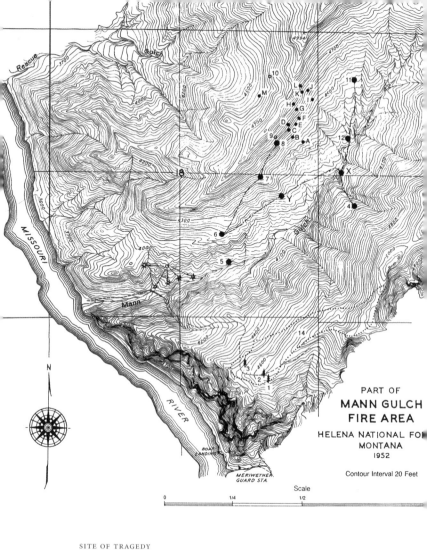

PART OF
**MANN GULCH
FIRE AREA**

HELENA NATIONAL FO
MONTANA
1952

Contour Interval 20 Feet

Scale

SITE OF TRAGEDY
The smokejumpers'
last desperate moments
are shown in this
map, which uses letters
to mark the points
at which each was
overcome by the fire.

Twenty miles north of Helena, Montana, the Missouri River flowing north cuts into the eastern slope of the Rocky Mountains on the first leg of its great, semicircular, 2,500-mile journey to meet the Mississippi. Lewis and Clark passed through this spectacular formation on July 19, 1805, and named it "Gates of the Mountains." Two miles downriver from the Gates, a small, two-mile-long canyon runs down to the Missouri from the northeast. This is Mann Gulch.

It is the site of a tragedy: the Mann Gulch fire. More than 50 years ago, on August 5, 1949, 13 young men—12 smokejumpers and one fireguard with the U.S. Forest Service—lost their lives here in a fire that did not behave as they expected it to. Although the disaster, the first one in which smokejumpers died, was headline news at the time, the story fell into relative obscurity until a book appeared. Called *Young Men and Fire*, it was written by Norman MacLean, a Shakespeare scholar and the author of *A River Runs Through It*. MacLean, who had fought forest fires as a young man, became obsessed with the Mann Gulch story, and spent two decades researching it.

His book was published in 1992, two years after his death at age 87.

Many of you have probably read *Young Men and Fire*. For those who haven't, let me briefly tell the story.

On the afternoon of August 4, 1949, a lightning storm started a small fire near the top of the southeast ridge of Mann Gulch — Meriwether Ridge, a slope forested with Douglas fir and ponderosa pine. The fire was spotted the next day; by 2:30 p.m., a C-47 transport plane had flown out of Missoula, Montana, carrying 16 smokejumpers. One got sick and didn't jump. The rest — 15 men between 17 and 33 years old — parachuted to the head of the gulch at 4:10 p.m. Their radio didn't make it. Its chute failed to open, and it crashed. They were joined on the ground by a fireguard, who had spotted the fire. Otherwise, the smokejumpers were isolated from the outside world.

The smokejumpers were a new organization, barely nine years old in 1949. Building in part on military experience from World War II, they were reinventing the approach to forest fire containment — aggressive, highly tactical, and coordinated. To them, the Mann Gulch fire, covering 60 acres at the time of the jump, appeared routine. It was what they called a "ten o'clock fire," meaning that they would have it beaten by ten o'clock in the morning of the day after they jumped.

They were wrong.

The first reconnaissance team headed down the south side of the gulch. The foreman, Wag Dodge, became worried that the group could get trapped on that side. He ordered them to come back and cross with the rest of the men to the north side of the gulch, opposite the fire, and head down the hill, so that the river, an escape route, would be at their backs as they fought the fire.

The north side of the gulch was grassland, covered in bunchgrass 30 inches tall, with almost no trees. It was unfamiliar terrain to these firefighters, who had been trained in the forests around Missoula.

Dodge was the first to spot the impending disaster — the fire had jumped the gulch from the south side to the north. It had ignited the grass only 200 yards ahead of the lead smokejumpers, blocking their route to the river. No one had seen the potential for this flanking action, since the downhill view was obstructed by a series of low ridges, and they had no detailed maps.

Now a race began. Dodge knew that the grassfire would cut off the route to the river, and would head swiftly up the north slope toward the firefighters. He ordered the group to reverse course immediately, and head back up the slope toward the ridge crest, hoping to get over it before the fire did.

The north slope of Mann Gulch is steep — a 76 percent slope on the average. Photos don't capture the reality. You have to go there to understand. It is hard even to walk up such a slope, but these young men were trying to run up it. Add air 100 degrees at the start and superheated by the rushing fire, add the poor visibility from smoke and airborne debris, add the weight of the packs and tools that these men were taught never to drop, and add their inexperience with the pace and heat of grassfires— far hotter and moving a lot faster than fires in forests. At 5:45 p.m., when the crew turned around, the fire was traveling toward them at 120 feet per minute, or 1.4 miles an hour. Ten minutes later, at 5:55 p.m., it was traveling at 610 feet per minute—seven miles an hour.

Wag Dodge knew they would lose the race to the top. With the fire barely 200 yards behind him, he did a strange and marvelous thing. He invented a solution. On the spot. His crew must have thought he had gone crazy as he took some matches out of his pocket, bent down, lit a match, and set fire to the grass directly in front of him. The new fire spread quickly uphill ahead of him, and he stepped into the middle of the newly burnt area. He called to his crew to join him as he lay down in the middle of the burnt ground. Dodge had invented what is now called an "escape fire," and soon after Mann Gulch it became a standard part of the training of all Forest Service firefighters.

But, on August 5, 1949, no one followed Wag Dodge. They ignored him, or they didn't hear him, and they ran right past the answer. The fire raged past Wag Dodge and overtook the crew. Only three made it to the top of the ridge, and one of the three was so badly burned that he died a few hours later. Of the 16 men who had fought the fire, three lived: Robert Sallee and Walter Rumsey, who made it over the crest, and Wag Dodge, who survived nearly unharmed in his escape fire.

When I first read *Young Men and Fire,* the story gripped me. I didn't understand why until I read a paper by Professor Karl E. Weick, of the University of Michigan. Weick is a student of organizations, especially organizations under stress, and even more especially organizations that are able to function well under trying conditions, the so-called high-reliability organizations, like aircraft carriers and the smokejumpers at their best. His paper is called, "The Collapse of Sensemaking in Organizations: The Mann Gulch Disaster." I want to review some of Weick's main points here, and then I will find my way—though you probably think I can't—back to health care.

Weick asks two questions about the Mann Gulch tragedy: Why did the smokejumpers' organization unravel? And, how can such organizations be made more resilient?

Weick regards the group of Mann Gulch smokejumpers as an organization, and he thinks that one of the key roles of organizations is what he calls "sensemaking." He has written a fine book called *Sensemaking in Organizations.* Sensemaking is the process through which the fluid, multilayered world is given order, within which people can orient themselves, find purpose, and take effective action. Weick is a postmodern thinker. He believes that there is little or no preexisting sense of organization in the world—that is, no order that comes before the definition of order. Organizations don't discover sense, they create it.

Weick tells the story of a reconnaissance group of soldiers lost in the Alps on a training mission. It was winter, they had no maps, and they seemed hopelessly lost. They were preparing to die, when one soldier found a map crushed down at the bottom of his pack. With the map in hand, they regained their courage, bivouacked for the night, and proceeded out of the mountains the next day to rescue. Only when they were recuperating in the main camp did someone notice that the map they had been using wasn't a map of the Alps at all; it was a map of the Pyrenees. Weick uses this story to point out that sensemaking is an act of its own, valuable in itself, and independent of any notion of reality. "This story raises the remarkable idea," he says, "that, when you are lost, any map will do."

In groups of interdependent people, organizations create sense out of possible chaos. Organizations unravel when sensemaking collapses, when they can no longer supply meaning, when they cling to interpretations that no longer work.

For the Mann Gulch smokejumpers, what appeared to be a small, manageable fire quickly turned into something unknown, and much more dangerous. Weick calls this sudden loss of meaning a "cosmology episode." The experience is fundamental and terrifying—the group, the roles, the interrelationships, the tools, the orderliness that the sensemaking organization had provided collapse, and people are left alone, unable to communicate with each other. They panic.

Weick supplies a "recipe" for the collapse of sensemaking:

> Thrust people into unfamiliar roles; leave some key roles unfilled; make the task more ambiguous; discredit the role system; and make all of these changes in a context in which small things can combine into something monstrous.

Now, maybe my route back to health care is becoming a little bit clearer.

Is health care unraveling? Are we in a cosmology episode?

In a recent survey of 42 medical group practices about morale among physicians and office staff, only 15 percent of the respondents rated their work environment as "good" or "excellent." Medicare and Medicaid managed care rolls are dropping monthly. We have tens of millions of uninsured Americans, significant medication errors in seven out of every 100 inpatients, tenfold or more variation in population-based rates of important surgical procedures, 30 percent overuse of advanced antibiotics, excessive waits throughout our system of care, 50 percent or more underuse of effective and inexpensive medications for heart attacks and immunization for the elderly, and declining service ratings from patients and their families. In 1998, the American Customer Satisfaction Index rated Americans' satisfaction with hospitals at 70 percent, just below the U.S. Postal Service (71%) and just above the Internal Revenue Service (69%). Racial gaps in health status remain enormous; a black male born in Baltimore today will, on the average, live eight years less than an average white male. All this happens with per capita health care costs 30 to 40 percent higher in the United States than in the next most expensive nation.

But, is the health care system *unraveling*? Isn't that going a bit too far?

I face a personal dilemma here. This has been a tough year for my family, and especially for my wife, Ann, who last spring began developing symptoms of a rare and serious autoimmune spinal cord problem. In early March, Ann competed in a 28-kilometer cross-country ski race in Alaska. Two months later, she couldn't walk across our bedroom. From April through September, Ann had six hospitalizations for a total of more than 60 inpatient days in three institutions, while she gradually experienced increasing pain, lost the ability to walk, and became essentially bedridden. For most of that time, nobody could tell us what exactly was happening or what her prognosis was. I can report some better news now, because Ann has clearly begun to improve. She can now walk long distances with a cane, and she is beginning to get back to her work, and she and I think she is going to be all right, though it will take a long time.

My dilemma is this: Our ordeal has been enormously painful and intensely private, and it is by no means over yet. To use it for any public purpose, even to speak about it, risks crossing a boundary of propriety and confidentiality that ought not to be crossed. And yet, this has been the formative experience for me overall in the past year—the experience of the decade—and it resonates so thoroughly with the mission of improving health care that not to learn from it also seems wrong.

I asked Ann for permission to speak about her illness, and she agreed. She and I both hope that some good can come of it.

Let me first say that this painful summer and fall have left me more impressed than I have ever been with the good will, kindness, generosity, commitment, and dignity of the people who work in health care—almost all of them.

Day after day and night after night, Ann, our children, and I have been deeply touched by acts of consideration, empathy, and technical expertise that these good people— nurses, doctors, technicians, housekeepers, dieticians, volunteers, and aides of all sorts—have brought to her bedside. The kindness crosses all boundaries. I asked Ann what she regards as the most impressive moments of help in her inpatient experience, and she mentions, first, a housekeeper who every evening would come into her room and, while cleaning, talk about her children and ours—a common humanity. Ann also remembers the young infectious disease fellow who, in the darkest of our hours, sat by Ann's bed and said what we were feeling: "Not knowing is the worst thing of all." Until then, no one had quite labeled this deep source of suffering.

For these incessant kindnesses, we are deeply grateful. We were fortunate, indeed, to have access to care in several of the finest hospitals in our nation.

Which makes it hard to tell the other side of the story, too. Put very, very simply: The people work well, by and large, but the system often does not. Every hour of our care reminded me, and alerted Ann, about the enormous, costly, and painful gaps between what we got in our days of need, and what we needed. The experience did not actually surprise me, but it did shock me. Put in other terms, as a friend of mine said: Before this, I was concerned; now, I am radicalized. If what happened to Ann could happen in our best institutions, I wonder more than ever before what the average must be like.

Above all, we needed safety, and yet Ann was unsafe. I have read the work of the physician Lucian Leape documenting medication errors, but now I have seen them firsthand, at the sharp end, sitting by Ann's bedside for week after week of acute care. The errors were not rare; they were the norm. During one admission, the neurologist told us in the morning, "By no means should you be getting anticholinergic agents," and a medication with profound anticholinergic side effects was given that afternoon. The attending neurologist in another admission told us by phone that a crucial and potentially toxic drug should be started immediately. He said, "Time is of the essence." That was on Thursday morning at 10:00 a.m. The first dose was given 60 hours later—Saturday night at 10:00 p.m. Nothing I could do, nothing I did, nothing I could think of made any difference. It nearly drove me mad. Colace was discontinued by a physician's order on Day 1, and was nonetheless brought by the nurse every single evening throughout a 14-day admission. Ann was supposed to receive five intravenous doses of a very toxic chemotherapy agent, but dose #3 was labeled as "dose #2." For half a day, no record could be found that dose #2 had ever been given, even though I had watched it drip in myself. I tell you from my personal observation: No day passed—not one—without a medication error. Most weren't serious, but they scared us.

We needed consistent, reliable information, based, we would have hoped, on the best science available. Instead, we often heard a cacophony of meaningless and sometimes contradictory conclusions. Ann received Cytoxan, which causes hair loss and low white blood cell count. *When would these occur?* we asked. The answers varied by a factor of five. Drugs tried and proven futile in one admission would be recommended in the next as if they were fresh ideas. A spinal tap was done for a test for Lyme disease, but the doctor collected too little fluid for the test, and the tap had to be repeated. During a crucial phase of diagnosis, one doctor told us to hope that the diagnosis would be of a certain disease, because that disease has a benign course. That same evening, another doctor told us to hope for the opposite, because that same disease is relentless—sometimes fatal. Complex, serial information on blood counts, temperature, functional status, and weight—the information on the basis of which risky and expensive decisions were relying—was collected in disorganized, narrative formats, embedded in nursing notes and daily forms. As far as I know, the only person who ever drew a graph of Ann's fevers or white blood cell counts was me, and the data were so complex and crossed so many settings that, short of a graph, no rational interpretation was possible. As a result, physicians often reached erroneous conclusions, such as assuming that Ann had improved after a specific treatment when, in fact, she had improved before it, or not at all. The experience of patienthood, or patient-spousehood, as the case may be, was often one of trying to get the attention of decision-makers to correct their impressions or their assumptions. Sociologically, this proved very tough, as we felt time and again our migration to the edge of the label "difficult patient."

We needed respect for our privacy, personal attention, and timely care. Often we got it. But often we didn't. On at least three occasions, Ann waited alone for over an hour, cold and frightened on a gurney in the waiting area outside an MRI unit in a sub-basement in the middle of the night. A nurse insisted that Ann swallow her pills while she watched, "because elderly patients sometime drop their medicines." Ann's bedtime was 10:00 p.m., but her sleeping medication was often brought at 8:00 p.m., to accommodate changes in nursing shifts. By Day 30 of hospitalization, Ann knew exactly which sleeping pills would work and which would not, and yet it was a daily struggle to get the right ones to her, as new clinicians insisted on trying their own approaches, ignoring Ann's expertise. One place gave a sleeping pill at 3:00 a.m., and then routinely woke Ann at 4:00 a.m. to take her blood pressure, which never varied from normal. An emergency room visit for a diagnostic spinal tap that should have taken two hours evolved into an 11-hour ordeal of constant delay.

In all of our hospitalizations, there have been only two instances when someone actively sought our feedback on the care system itself. Only two people ever asked us to make suggestions about how their system could be improved.

We needed continuity. Ann's story was extremely complex, and evolved over many weeks. And yet we often felt that the only real memories in the system were ours. Times of transition of responsibility, such as the first of the month, were especially trying. On one "first of the month," the new senior attending physician walked into Ann's room, cheerfully introduced himself, and asked, "So how long have you had MS?" Ann doesn't have MS. Over and over and over again Ann had to tell her story, longer and more complex as time passed. By the fifth or tenth or fifteenth iteration, any plausibility to the common explanation—"fresh minds, two heads are better than one"—gave way to our doubts that any of these caring people ever talked to each other at all. "Discharge" from a hospital really meant it. I would estimate that 50 different doctors and three times as many nurses became closely involved with Ann's care in hospitals—intensely involved. And yet, to my knowledge, only three of these individuals made any effort to follow Ann's course after any particular discharge, and these three are actively managing Ann's outpatient care at this time. The rest have, I suspect, no way at all to know how she is faring, or whether their diagnoses and prognoses were, after all, correct. Continuity, when it occurred, was based on acts of near heroism. Ann's primary neurologist travels frequently for speaking engagements. When he was away during crucial times, he phoned Ann every day, whether from Amsterdam, London, Geneva, or San Francisco.

One after another, caregivers told us of their own distress. The occupational therapist apologized for cutting back Ann's treatment, explaining that 17 OTs had been laid off the week before. The doctors told us about insurance forms and fights for needed hospital days. The nurses complained that the transport service never came.

And the bills were astounding. They have been covered by our insurance, for which we are immensely grateful. But I cannot reconcile what happened with the fees. Pharmacy charges of $30 for a single pill. Remember the Colace that was discontinued but brought anyway? Well, there it is: Pill by pill charges for all the days on which the nurse opened the unneeded packet and threw it in the garbage. Radiology charges of $155 per film for second readings of 14 films transferred from one hospital to another. MRI scans over and over again for $1,700, $2,000, $2,200 per procedure. Ann's care has been billed at perhaps $150,000 so far, at a minimum, and the bare fact is that, of all that enormous investment, a remarkably small percentage—half at best, probably much less—stood any chance at all of helping her. The rest has been pure waste. Even while simpler needs, for a question answered, information explained, a word of encouragement, or just good and nourishing food, have gone unmet.

Not all of these flaws in care were equally present in all of the hospitals. Some were much better than others. In fact, if we could combine the best of care in each, we would have a system far closer to ideal. But some of these defects existed everywhere, and this was in some of the best hospitals in America.

I am deeply, deeply grateful for the people, and I respect the institutions a great deal. But we have so much left to do. We are causing harm, and we need to stop it. I think the fire has jumped the gulch. The blaze is on our side. As I waited helplessly for Ann to get a medicine when "time was of the essence," I even felt the fire licking at my heels.

The people know this. Not just the people in the beds, but the people doing the work, too. The doctors and nurses and technicians and managers and pharmacists and all the rest know—*they must know*—the truth.

They see it every day, and even if their defensive routines no longer permit them to say what they see, they do see it: errors, delays, nonsensical variation, lack of communication, misinformation, the care environment not at all a place of healing.

"Why do organizations unravel?" asks Karl Weick. "Because they no longer make sense of the world," he answers. I love medicine. I love the purpose of our work. But we are unraveling, I think. Sense is collapsing.

And yet, this does not need to happen. Sensemaking is within our reach. Karl Weick asks a second question, with much more embedded optimism: "How can organizations be made more resilient?"

He answers that resilience has four sources in organizations, equipping them to, in his words, "forestall deterioration" of their sensemaking function.

First, there is "improvisation," the ability to invent when old formulas fail. The young men at Mann Gulch had been trained to never, under any circumstances, drop their tools. One of their tools was a Pulaski, a combination axe and pick that is very useful in fighting forest fires. It's not useful to carry it up a 76 percent slope when a grassfire is racing toward you at 610 feet per minute. And yet, the reconstructed journeys of the victims of the fire show that several carried their Pulaskis a good way up the hill as they raced for their lives. Wag Dodge, in the midst of ultimate crisis, improvised the escape fire, though no one followed him.

Second, there are what Weick calls "virtual role systems." These systems refer to the ability of individuals to carry, as it were, a social system inside their heads—to assume structures even when they are not externally apparent. If the smokejumper crew had still seen Wag Dodge as their leader when he invented his escape fire, maybe they would have followed him. They didn't: The smoke and fear and noise and shock had not only disrupted the smokejumper system as a formal entity, it had also disrupted its representation in the mind of each individual. The organization could have been preserved if individual minds had held on to it, but they did not. The system fragmented, and the roles disappeared.

Third, says Weick, resilience within an organization is maintained by "the attitude of wisdom." He quotes John Meacham, who writes, "Ignorance and knowledge grow together.... To be wise is not to know particular facts but to know without excessive confidence or excessive cautiousness.... [In changing times] organizations most need ... curiosity, openness, and complex sensing."

Fourth and finally, Weick says, resilience requires "respectful interaction." "If a role system collapses among people for whom trust, honesty, and self-respect are underdeveloped," Weick maintains, "then they are on their own. And fear often swamps their resourcefulness. If, however, a role system collapses among people where trust, honesty, and self-respect are more fully developed, then new options … are created."

I think that this idea — the loss of sensemaking — is a powerful vocabulary for interpreting the health care crisis of our time. At least it captures the most disturbing aspects of what Ann and I experienced this year. If I'm right, then it might lead us to new ideas that are every bit as tough to embrace as Wag Dodge's escape fire, and every bit as promising. I want to imagine health care's escape fire, and I want to be bold.

I have decided to divide the question into two parts. It seems to me that the health care system's capacity to preserve sensemaking in a time of crisis requires change at two levels. I call them preconditions and designs.

Preconditions are a set of shared assumptions that don't tell us what future we need to build, but that give us a chance of staying in order long enough to tackle that issue. They make sense possible.

Designs are the basic ideas behind the escape fire itself. These are the new ways of thinking about what we do. The new sense. The scheme we create together to organize a world that threatens otherwise to become chaotic and overtake us.

I can see five preconditions that give us a chance at sensemaking.

The first is the toughest: We need to face reality. This is very, very hard. Why did it take the Mann Gulch crew so long to realize they were in trouble? The soundest explanation is not that the threat was too small to see; it is that it was too big. Some problems are too overwhelming to name. I now think that that is where we have come in health care; I *have* been radicalized. Our challenge is not to develop more sensitive ways to detect our risks, our errors, our flaws, our variation, our indignities, our fragmentation, our delays, our waste, our insults to the people we say we exist to serve. Our challenge is to have the courage to name clearly and boldly the problems we have— many—at the size they occupy—immense. We must find ways to do this without either marginalizing the truth-teller or demoralizing the good people working in these bad systems.

David Lawrence, former CEO of Kaiser Permanente Foundation Health Plan, has said it best. He said, "The chassis is broken." Our challenges are not marginal and their solutions are not incremental. The sooner we get honest about those facts, the sooner we can get on with the job.

The second precondition is that we drop the Pulaskis. Our current tools can't do the job. We can't get where we need to go by stressing the current system. You can't possibly run fast enough up a 76 percent slope.

Let me show you the difference. At the Institute for Healthcare Improvement, we have two bathrooms. Each has a sign on the door that can be set in two positions: "vacant" or "occupied." You flip the sign as you enter and leave. Or, you don't. In 71 observations, I obtained the following data. The sign was correct 43 out of 71 times, or 61 percent of the time. It was wrong 39 percent of the time. The most common error, 30 percent of the time, was that the sign said "occupied" when the room was actually vacant. This error causes moderate to severe discomfort in timid staff members who do not check the door handle. The other error, 10 percent of the time, was that the sign said "vacant" when the room was actually occupied. This error can cause injury if a staff member tries to pull the door and it is locked, or embarrassment if they trust the sign and the occupant has forgotten to lock the door.

The sign system functions poorly. In fact, if you simply guessed that the room was vacant, you would have been right 44 times out of 71, or 62 percent of the time—more often than the sign.

I decided to fix the system by emphasizing it. Here is my reminder sign. It never lasted more than an hour

PLEASE FLIP
THE SIGN

PLEASE READ THE
SIGN (BELOW) ABOUT
FLIPPING THE SIGN!

PLEASE FLIP
THE SIGN

before someone tore it down. I tried to highlight its importance by making a sign for the sign for the sign, but that, too, was torn down. The experiment ended with a surge of graffiti, which I thought lacked taste.

Such an approach will never work. On the other hand, you and I have both been in airplanes with a lavatory sign system that is right nearly 100 percent of the time. The reason is that the locking system in airplane lavatories uses a design principle called a "forcing function." It doesn't allow for choice—you can't lock the door or turn on the light without changing the sign. And you can't open the door without changing the sign again.

Our health care escape fire will have the same principles. It will not just invoke different tools, it will force us to drop the old ones. Health care's backpack is full of useless assumptions so old and often repeated that they have become wisdom from the mouth of Hippocrates himself, and one questions them at grave risk to one's professional relationships.

Precondition number three is that we "stay in formation." Weick refers to this as having virtual role models. In the Mann Gulch fire, the organization disappeared at the moment of crisis. It became every man for himself. Nobody remembered that Wag Dodge was the most experienced and the leader, or that together the crew might learn something that separately they could not. The men's bodies afterward were literally strewn for 300 yards across the slope.

Successful sensemaking can't leave anyone out. Health care's disintegration is not yet every man for himself, but it is every discipline for itself, every guild for itself. As a result, we tend to assume today that one guild's solution cannot be another's. We assume that either we will preserve quality or cut costs; that patients will get what they ask for or that science will prevail; that managers will run the show or that doctors will be in control; that the bottom line is financial or moral.

This won't work. No comprehensive solution is possible if it fails to make sense to any of the key stakeholders. At least four parts of our crew need to share in the solution—a common answer—or the crew will fall apart. Whatever escape fire we create has to make sense in the world of science and professionalism, in the world of the patient and family, in the world of the business and finance of health care, and in the world of the good, kind people who do the work of caring. I think the toughest part of this may be in terms of the business and financing of care. There is a tendency to assume that financial success—e.g., thriving organizations—and great care are mutually exclusive. However, we will not make progress unless and until these goals become aligned with each other.

The fourth precondition is procedural: To achieve sense, we have to talk to each other, and listen. Sensemaking is fundamentally an enterprise of interdependency, and the currency of interdependency is conversation. In the noise and smoke of the fire, just at the time when our interdependency is most crucial, it becomes most difficult to communicate. This will not do. Civil, open dialogue is a precondition for success.

The fifth, and final, precondition for success I can see is leadership. You don't achieve sense without having leaders. Effective leaders in high-reliability organizations exhibit certain skills: clearly defining tasks; demonstrating their own competence; disavowing perfection so as to encourage openness; and engaging and building the team. Leadership like this makes constructive, informed interactions more likely and, at a deeper level, leaves the sensemaking apparatus intact as the context changes.

I believe that these five preconditions—facing reality, dropping the old tools, staying in formation, communicating, and having capable leadership—set the stage for making sense as the fire blows up. Now we have a chance. What does the escape fire look like?

I think that health care's escape fire has three primary design elements. None is totally new, but together, fully realized, they would create a care system that is as different from today's as a 76 percent slope is from an escape fire. I will call these elements access, science, and relationships.

"Access" refers to the property of a system that promises, "We are there for you." The current system of care embeds processes and assumptions that ration, limit, and control access. To get help requires appointments, permission, authorization, waiting, forms, and procedures to which the person in need must bend their need. In the current system, *first* we allocate the supply, and *then* we experience the demand. We accept as inevitable that accessibility at some times—weekends, nights, holidays—is of course different from 9 to 5. Demand often feels unpredictable, threatening, and even hostile, and we reply with equal unpredictability, threat, and counter-accusations about insatiable patients and unrealistic expectations.

All of this changes in the escape fire. The new system of access can be summarized in one phrase: "24/7/365." The access to help that we will envision is uncompromising, meeting whatever need exists, whenever and wherever it exists, in whatever form requested.

Before the howling starts, let me remind you of one precondition: Drop your Pulaskis. 24/7/365 is not at all achievable with the current tools. Meeting demand this well within current frameworks is harder than running a marathon up a 76 percent grade. It cannot be done.

Our Pulaski in the search for access is the encounter —the visit. Total access 24/7/365 begins to be achievable only when we agree—scientists, professionals, patients, payers, and the health care workforce—that the product we choose to make is not visits. Our product is healing relationships, and these can be fashioned in many new and wonderful forms if we suspend the old ways of making sense of care.

The access we need to create is access to help and healing, and that does not always mean—in fact, I think it rarely means—reliance on face-to-face meetings between patients, doctors, and nurses. Tackled well, I believe that this new framework will gradually reveal that half or more of our encounters—maybe as many as 80 percent of them—are neither wanted by patients nor deeply believed in by professionals. This is an example of a problem so big that we have trouble seeing it. The health care encounter as a face-to-face visit is a dinosaur. More exactly, it is a form of relationship of immense and irreplaceable value to a few of the people we seek to help, and these few have their access severely curtailed by the use of visits to meet the needs of many, whose needs could be better met through other kinds of encounters.

The alternatives to visits in the escape fire are many: self-care strongly supported and unequivocally encouraged; group visits of patients with like needs, with or without professionals involved; Internet use for access to scientific and popular information; e-mail care between patients and clinicians; and well-managed chat rooms, electronic and real, for patients and significant others who face common challenges.

Payers should take careful note: Most of you still pay only for Pulaskis. The greatest potential for reducing costs while maintaining and improving the lot of patients is to replace visits with better, more flexible and fine-tuned forms of care. But almost all current payment mechanisms, whether enforced by the market or mapped into organizations by internal compensation systems, use impoverished definitions of productivity that actively discourage the search for and incorporation of non-visit care.

Another form of access is access to one's own medical information; it, too, is a form of non-visit care. An employee of the Institute for Healthcare Improvement recently had a test for a potentially serious disease. She called the clinical office for the result, and heard the following: "Yes, Ms. Smith…your result is right here. It is…uh-oh…ah…Ms. Smith, I am not authorized to give you this information. You will need to talk with the doctor. He will be back tomorrow." When my wife was on Cytoxan, she and I were the only people who were actually tracking her white blood cell count graphically, and yet several of her nurses refused to tell us the white count results when they became available.

The medical record properly belongs to the patient, not to the care system. It must become an open book to the patient, available without restriction, hesitation, or suspicion. Diane Plamping, a public health researcher from the U.K., offered me the following rule about access to information: "Nothing about me without me."

In my escape fire, we will have a new view of the nature of information in health care. In the current model, information is treated generally as a tool for retrospection, a record of what has happened, a stable asset that we may or may not use to recall the past, or to defend or prosecute a lawsuit.

Here in my escape fire, the view of information is different. Information, we now see, *is* care. People want knowledge, and the transfer of knowledge is caring, itself.

Whenever we put a block or bottleneck in the way of knowledge transfer—whether we call it an appointment, or permission, or even a decision by anyone other than the person who wants to know—we add cost without value and fail to meet need. We also put 24/7/365 even further from our reach.

I recently visited a magnificent new hospital, which has developed a state-of-the-art health information library for patients. There were computer terminals everywhere, user-friendly books, three-dimensional models, and a full collection of instructional videotapes. I spoke to the nurse who ran the library, and she complained that it was vastly underutilized because they were having a hard time getting doctors to send their patients there.

I asked, "Why not go directly to the patients and get the doctors out of the loop?"

She said, "The doctors would never go for that."

I wanted to say, "Come into my escape fire. In here, we know that information is a form of care, and that doctors' visits and decisions are, too. And we want to make sure that anyone who needs either gets it. Doctors are useful for some forms of caring; information resources like yours are useful for others."

So, the first element of my escape fire is total access, without compromise: 24/7/365.

The second element is science. At its best, the help we offer is based in knowledge. When care matches knowledge, it is most reliable. When care does not match knowledge, we fail to help, either by omission (failing to do what would help) or by waste (doing what cannot help). The current world is far too tolerant of mismatches between knowledge and action, far too permissive of omission and waste. As a result, our care is unreliable, our answers are inconsistent, and our practices vary without sense.

The escape fire looks different. I urge here that we adopt Dr. James Reinertsen's formulation: "All and only." "We will promise to deliver, reliably and without error, all the care that will help, and only the care that will help."

The Pulaski here may be an illogical commitment to the autonomy of clinical decisions. Just as the hospital with the patients' library illogically places the doctor between the patient and the information the patient wants, so the system fundamentally committed to autonomy places the individual doctor's mind between the patient and the best knowledge anywhere. Doctor visits are irreplaceable, sometimes; so is a doctor's autonomy to assure that the patient is well served. But, in my escape fire, I would place a commitment to excellence—standardization to the best-known method—above clinician autonomy as a rule for care.

Physicians stand only to gain from this change of perspective. They know, as I do, that the volume of scientific medical literature today far outpaces the capacity of any one doctor—any 100 doctors—to stay up-to-date. Dr. Larry Weed—a physician and a specialist in medical informatics—says that asking an individual doctor to rely on his memory to store and retrieve all the facts relevant to patient care is like asking travel agents to memorize airline schedules. The art of the physician is to synthesize many different sources of information; this art should be used exactly and only when less expensive, less creative resources will not suffice.

This issue does not begin with a commitment to artificial intelligence or knowledge management. It begins with a commitment to standardize excellence.

This includes a commitment to safety for patients and for staff. By some calculations, the aviation industry's safety record is better than health care's by a factor of 1,000 or more. And aviation safety has improved tenfold in the past three decades, during a period of massive growth in volume and technology. This has been accomplished through science, not through exhortation. There are safe designs and there are unsafe designs. The issue has very little to do with the will or capability of human beings, who almost never intend errors to happen. It has a lot to do with whether leaders, board members, and

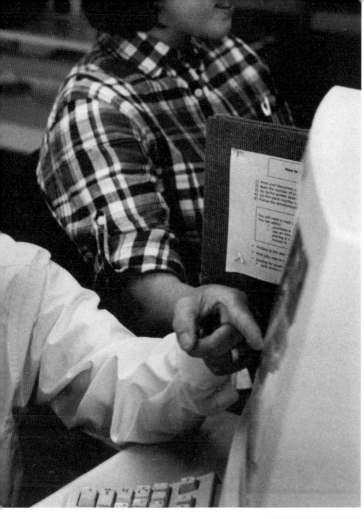

INFORMATION ACCESS
A cardiology patient at
the University of Colorado
Health Sciences Center
reviews his electronic
medical record with Chen-
Tan Lin, MD, as part
of a study of information
access and its value.

managers employ the best available knowledge about safe designs for tasks, equipment, rules, and environments instead of relying on outmoded traditions and impoverished theories about motivation and "trying harder."

A scientific system of care would guarantee that the best-known approach is the standard approach.

The third element of the escape fire I will call "relationships" or, perhaps, "interactions." While the first element, access, encourages us to consider how people get to the help they need, and the second, science, asks us to consider how we can assure that the best knowledge informs action, the interactions element challenges our current notions of the very nature of help, itself. It raises the question of what, in the end, we are spending $1 trillion to produce. It is about our purposes.

In Mann Gulch, the transition of purpose was stark and total—from defeating a ten o'clock fire to saving lives. Until that event, the smokejumpers' training and intent were focused almost entirely on the first task, and very little on the second. They felt invincible. After Mann Gulch, it became clear to all that smokejumper safety and survival was a task on its own, and the most important one.

In the current framework, health care tends to regard human interactions more as a toll or price than as a goal or product. The system tends to act as if interactions were the burden it must bear so that it can deliver the care. As a result, behaviors and systems emerge to control or limit interactions—as if they were a form of waste—and to regard commitment to interaction as a secondary issue in training, resource allocation, hiring, firing, and incentive.

In the escape fire, we see it differently. Here, we know that interaction is not the price of care; it is care, itself. A patient with a question presents an opportunity, not a burden. Time spent in building patients' skills in self-care is not a way to shift care, it *is* care. Access to information is desirable not because it improves care or supports compliance, but because it is a form of care.

University of Michigan education professor David Cohen says that no education occurs until what he calls "inert" assets (books, teachers, rooms, curricula, rules, budgets, and so on) interact with each other and with students. Education is interaction. People in educational organizations, he says, often behave as if the inert assets were essential and the interactions expendable. They fight political wars over budgets, space, and personnel, and spend little time defending and perfecting the interactions among these assets through cooperation, communication, teamwork, and knowledge about students.

It is the same in health care. Care is not doctors, nurses, hospitals, computers, books, rules, or medicines. These are inert. Care is interaction among our assets and between assets and patients. To perfect care, we must perfect interactions.

Four properties of interaction ought to be objects of investment and continual improvement in the escape fire. The first we have already covered: to regard information transfer as a key form of care, and to increase the accessibility, openness, reliability, and completeness of information for patients and families. Generic, scientific, and patient information should be available to them without restriction or delay. "Nothing about me without me" is a formula for idealized interaction just as it is for idealized access.

Second, interactions should be tailored to patients' needs. The call to arms here comes to me from a friend named Art Berarducci, who, when he was CEO of a small hospital, placed over the entrance a sign that read: "Every patient is the only patient." Each person in need brings to us a unique set of qualities that require unique responses. The overall list of such qualities may be familiar: comfort, dignity, communication, privacy, involvement of loved ones, respect for cultural and ethnic differences, need for control and sharing in decisions, and so on. But, for each individual, "quality of care" means balancing these various needs at levels that only the individual patient can determine. In the escape fire, we are not finished—we have not achieved excellence—until each individual is well served according to his or her needs, not ours. Our measure of successful interaction is not just an average of how we have done in the past for "them," but also the answer to the inquiry, "How did I just do for you?"

Third, interactions in the escape fire begin with this assumption: The patient is the source of all control. We act only when the patient grants that privilege, each time. The current system—the one ablaze—often behaves as if control over decisions, resources, access, and information begins in the hands of the caregivers, and is only ceded to patients when the caregivers choose to do so.

My wife had a surgical procedure and awoke in the recovery room asking for me. I was not permitted to join her for almost 90 minutes, even though she repeatedly asked that I be allowed to comfort her. Why did that staff and that institution willfully separate a man and his wife at a time when they could have offered support to one another? By what right does a nurse, doctor, or manager make a decision that violates basic principles of human decency and caring? As a husband and as a physician, I know that the rationale for asserting that right stands on infirm ground. In any other setting, such an act would be obviously wrong. In this one, it is less obvious, but it is still wrong.

Control begins in the hands of the people we serve. If we caregivers wish to take it, we must ask. If a patient denies control, then we must accept their will as a matter of right. We are not hosts in our organizations so much as we are guests in our patients' lives.

Finally, the interactions we nurture should be transparent. People often say that health care needs more "accountability." I have never quite known what that means. But I do understand the notion of transparency, and why it may help in the sensemaking process, and perhaps better achieve what those who urge accountability mean to have. In the old world, burning now, there is a premium on secrecy. The highly desirable goal of confidentiality has mutated into a monstrous system of closed doors and locked cabinets. "Nothing about me without me" has a necessary correlate: "I can discover what affects me." Health care should be confidential, but the health care industry is not entitled to secrecy.

The burden of reporting that has arisen in a world burning with conflict and mistrust has cast transparency in its most negative light. And yet I cannot imagine a future health care system in which we do not work in daylight, study openly what we do, and offer patients any windows they want onto the work that affects them. "No secrets" is the new rule in my escape fire.

These are the elements of my escape fire, first draft. I envision a system in which we promise those who depend on us total access to the help they need, in the form they need, when they need it. Our system will promise freedom from the tyranny of individual visits with overburdened professionals as the only way to find a healing relationship; will promise excellence as the standard, valuing such excellence over ill-considered autonomy; will promise safety; and will be capable of nourishing interactions in which information is central, quality is individually defined, control resides with patients, and trust blooms in an open environment.

It is a new system, and a lot of the old tools won't work anymore. Those who cling to their old tools and allow our organization to disintegrate will find little sense either in the burning present or in the challenging future. For them, sensemaking will have failed, and the panic of isolation will drive them up a slope that is too far and too steep for them to make it. For the rest, the possibility of invention and the opportunity to make sense—new sense—will open not just routes of escape, but vistas of achievement, that the old order could never have imagined.

# About the Author

Donald M. Berwick, MD, MPP, is president, CEO, and cofounder of the Institute for Healthcare Improvement (IHI) in Boston. IHI is a not-for-profit organization dedicated to improving the quality of health care systems through education, research, and demonstration projects, and through fostering collaboration among health care organizations and their leaders. Dr. Berwick is a clinical professor of pediatrics and health care policy at Harvard Medical School. He is also a pediatrician, an associate in pediatrics at Boston's Children's Hospital, and a consultant in pediatrics at Massachusetts General Hospital.

An internationally recognized expert on health care quality improvement, Dr. Berwick has published extensively in professional journals in the areas of health care policy, decision analysis, technology assessment, and health care quality management.

# About the Institute
# for Healthcare Improvement

The Institute for Healthcare Improvement (IHI) is a not-for-profit organization dedicated to improving the quality of health care in the United States and around the world. Founded in 1991 and based in Boston, Massachusetts, IHI develops, demonstrates, and draws attention to the most effective strategies for improving health care and fosters collaborations among health care organizations and their leaders to put those strategies into place.

Employing a staff of more than 50 people and maintaining partnerships with over 200 faculty members, IHI offers comprehensive products and services that facilitate demonstrable improvement in health care organizations. The goal is to close the gap between what is known to be the best care and the care that is actually delivered.